Mathstraks 7-8

Fun Number Activities
Lesley Higgin

Tarquin Group
www.tarquingroup.com

Publisher's Note

Lesley Higgin's tried and tested activities in this volume will enliven hundreds of classrooms and homework sessions across the world.

An experienced teacher and author, she brings practicality and a sense of fun to what can often seem dull learning and reinforcement tasks.

Junior Mathstraks are available in book and ebook form covering ages 8-9, 9-10, 10-11 and Extension for ages 10-11 - as well as this volume.

In addition there are Mathstraks volumes for early Secondary years on Algebra, Geometry and Number.

You can keep up to date with this and other new titles, special offers and more, through registering on our website for our e-mail newsletter or following us on Twitter or Facebook.

Published by Tarquin Publications
Suite 74, 17 Holywell Hill
St Albans
AL1 1DT

www.tarquingroup.com

Distributed in the USA by Parkwest
www.parkwestpubs.com
www.amazon.com & major retailers

Distributed in Australia by OLM www.lat-olm.com.au

Copyright © Lesley Higgin, 2016
ISBN 978-1-907550-76-8
ISBN 978-1-911093-26-8

Printed and designed in the United Kingdom

Introduction

It's always a challenge to be able to provide enough opportunity for children to practise number work, without them getting bored with repetitive exercises. I hope that this book will help.

I have developed the Mathstraks series to enable pupils to gain a solid understanding of numeracy through fun, challenge and play.

There are lots of different activities to enable children to use their number skills in a variety of situations, including puzzles, problem-solving and games. I have enjoyed writing the tasks and they have worked extremely well with my classes.

I hope you find the book useful and , most importantly, that the children enjoy it.

Lesley Higgin

Make Ten

On the following grid, try to find lines of 3 numbers which add together to make 10.

The lines may be horizontal, vertical or diagonal.

Draw a line through each group you find.

2	1	8	1	5
2	7	9	6	1
7	2	5	3	1
3	3	4	4	2
6	4	1	7	9
6	2	9	1	2
7	8	1	3	8

You will know when you have found them all!

Challenge!

Try to find all the possible ways of making 10 by adding 3 numbers.

Make Twenty

On the following grid, try to find lines of 3 numbers which add together to make 20.

The lines may be horizontal, vertical or diagonal.

Draw a line through each group you find.

5	1	2	7	19	10	3	9
11	3	13	1	18	5	2	6
4	4	12	9	9	8	10	3
6	9	7	6	1	1	9	5
1	9	10	3	6	12	7	5
5	16	4	7	1	8	5	9
3	7	3	14	3	11	12	8

Name the shapes you have found!

Challenge!

Try to find all the possible ways of making 20 by adding 3 numbers.

Celebrity Dance!

On a popular TV show, celebrities are judged as they learn to dance. They are given four scores, which are each out of 10.

A.   Work out the missing scores or total for each celebrity:

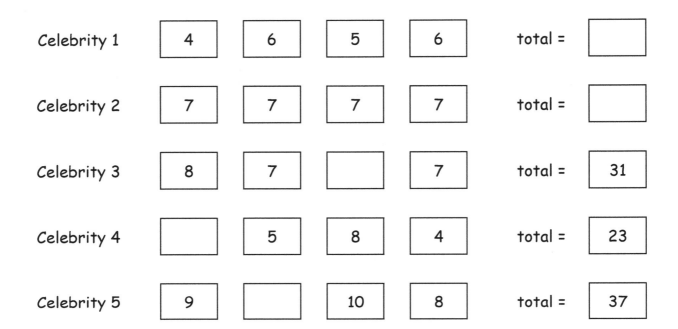

Celebrity 1	4	6	5	6	total =	
Celebrity 2	7	7	7	7	total =	
Celebrity 3	8	7		7	total =	31
Celebrity 4		5	8	4	total =	23
Celebrity 5	9		10	8	total =	37

B. Use the following clues to work out the scores for celebrities 6, 7, 8, 9 and 10.

▶ Celebrity 6 scored a total of 32. Each judge gave the same score.

▶ Celebrity 7 scored all 6's and 7's. The total score was 25.

▶ Celebrity 8 scored one 5. The other three scores were the same as each other. The total was 26.

▶ Celebrity 9 scored a total of 16. Each score was different. All four scores were odd.

▶ Celebrity 10 scored only even numbers. Each number was different. The total was 20.

Addition Grids

In the following addition grids, the numbers 2, 3, 4, 5, 6, 7, 8, 9 have each been used once in the shaded boxes. Work out which number goes where and then complete the rest of the grid.

A

+				
7	10		12	
	12	15		17
			9	

B

+				8
	13		7	
			8	
				15
	11			10

C

+				
		13	15	
		9		7
5	7		13	

Challenge!

In C, what do all the numbers inside the grid (not the shaded numbers) have in common?

Why has this happened?

Colour the Number

▶ This is a pen and paper version of the traditional game, 'Shut the Box'.

▶ Each player starts by drawing out the following grid:

1	2	3	4	5	6	7	8	9
			Score					

▶ Player 1 throws 2 six-sided dice and adds the two numbers.

▶ The player now tries to make this number by using any combination of numbers on their 1 to 9 grid. These number(s) are coloured on the grid. (A number may only be coloured once.) For example, If the player throws a 6 they may colour in any one of the following combinations:

6 or 1,5 or 2,4 or 3,6 or 1,2,3

▶ Player 1 carries on throwing dice and colouring in until they can no longer make the required number. The uncoloured numbers are then added. This is the player's score.

▶ Player 2 now has their turn. The winner is the player with the lowest score.

▶ Players can continue playing until one has a score of zero. This player is the ultimate winner!

Challenge Questions

1. Paul throws 12 and colours two numbers. What two numbers might he colour?

2. Sue has only the number '1' uncoloured on her grid. Can she become the ultimate winner on her next throw? Explain your answer.

3. Rob and Hannah have different tactics. Rob throws a '9' on his first go and he colours the number '9'. When Hannah throws a '9' on her first go, she colours the numbers 2, 3 and 4. Which tactic do you think is the best? Explain your answer.

Sum Arrows

Move around the following grids, filling in the answers as you go.

A. When you move right add 20. When you move up add 4.

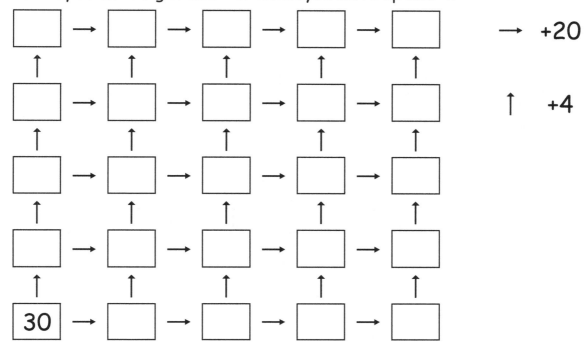

B. When you move right add 30. When you move up add 7.

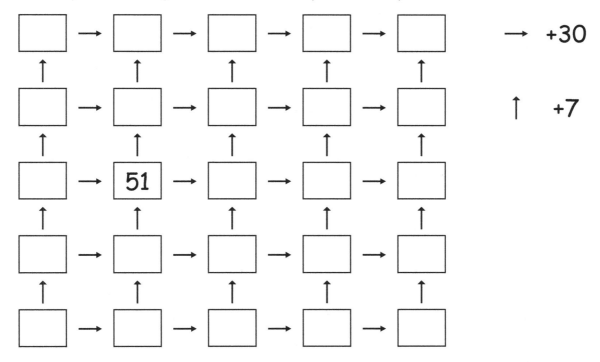

Wizard Maze

Sumsgalore the Wizard has to get through the mathematical maze without getting caught by the Terrible Trolls. Calculate your way around the maze. Only correct answers will lead you to safety!

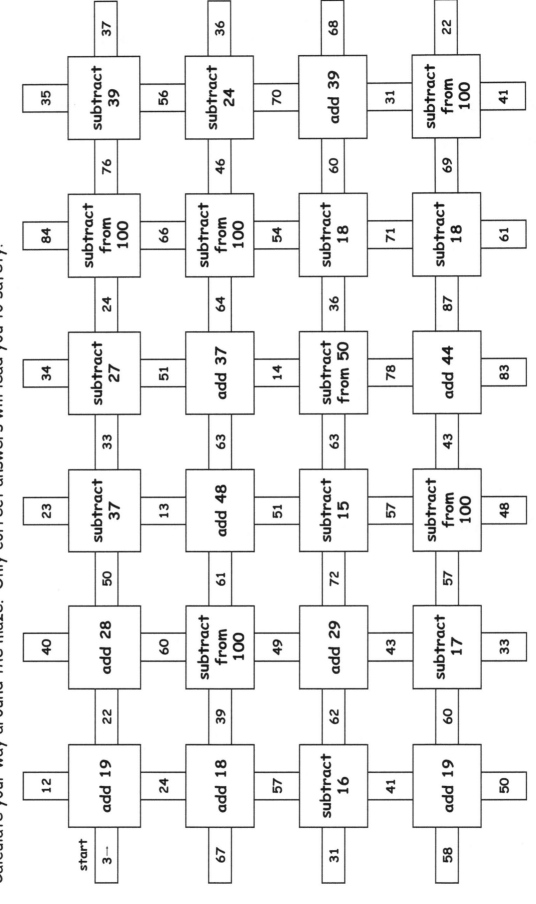

Sums and Differences

The **sum** of two numbers is found by adding them.

The **difference** of two numbers is found by subtracting the smallest from the largest.

Work out the missing numbers in the following grids like this:

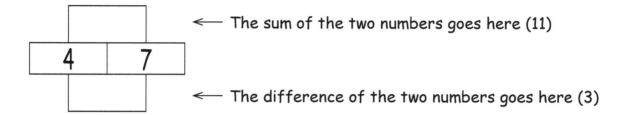

←— The sum of the two numbers goes here (11)

←— The difference of the two numbers goes here (3)

1.

| 19 | 7 |

2.

| 23 | 41 |

3.

| 49 | 36 |

4.

68
| 25 | |

5.

77
| | 18 |

6.

10
| | |
4

7.

15
| | |
1

8.

30
| | |
6

9.

100
| | |
50

Find a Fiver

Cut out the following squares.

Match them so that each pair of adjacent sides add up to £5.

£2.50	70p	£2.80
£2.30 **A** 40p	£4.70 **B** £1	£1.40 **C** £1.70
£1.30	£2.50	50p
£4.50	£2	10p
60p **D** £2.40	£3.50 **E** 30p	20p **F** £1.50
£1.60	£3.90	£2.20
£1.10	£3.70	£3.80
£3.30 **G** £2.70	90p **H** £1.80	£2.60 **I** £4.10
£1.20	£1.90	80p

Sequences

The following sequences are made by adding the same number again and again.

Fill in the boxes (even the shaded ones) to complete each sequence.

Describe each sequence in words.

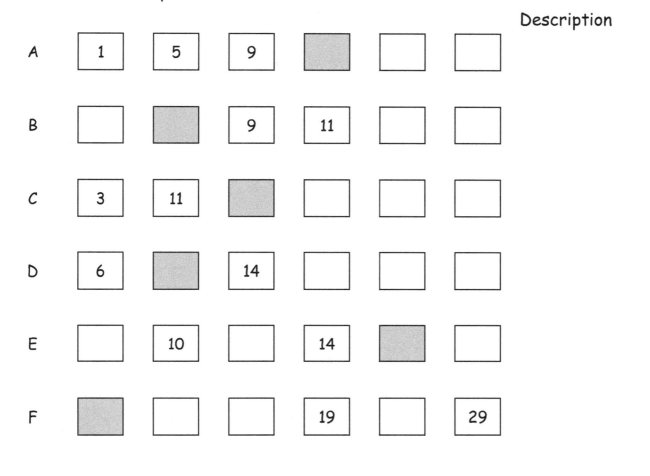

Description

A | 1 | 5 | 9 | | | |

B | | | 9 | 11 | | |

C | 3 | 11 | | | | |

D | 6 | | 14 | | | |

E | | 10 | | 14 | | |

F | | | | 19 | | 29 |

Write the numbers in the shaded boxes in the spaces below so that they are ordered smallest to largest.

This should form another sequence. Describe the sequence.
What are the next 3 terms?

Treasure Hunt

Each pirate has buried their treasure at the end of a sequence of numbers.

Follow each sequence and find the treasure! You may go from number to number horizontally, vertically or diagonally.

Write the name of each pirate next to their treasure.

One-eye Guy has buried his treasure starting at 3 and adding on 5's.

Captain Cath has buried her treasure starting at 0 and adding on 7's.

Blonde Beard has buried his treasure starting at 6 and adding on 2's.

Toothless Tina has buried her treasure starting at 24 and subtracting 4's.

Cut-throat Ken has buried his treasure starting at 9 and adding on 3's.

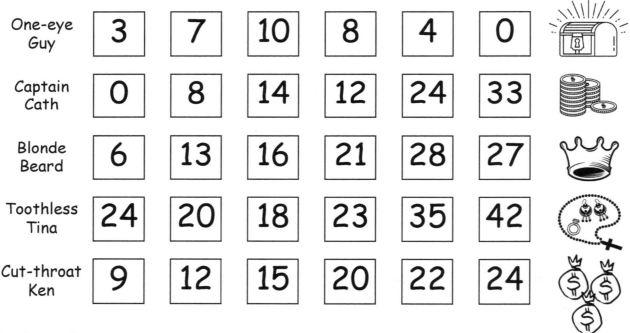

One-eye Guy	3	7	10	8	4	0
Captain Cath	0	8	14	12	24	33
Blonde Beard	6	13	16	21	28	27
Toothless Tina	24	20	18	23	35	42
Cut-throat Ken	9	12	15	20	22	24

Challenge!

Another pirate follows a sequence which starts at 5 and goes up in 2's. The treasure is buried at number 18. How long will it take the pirate to reach the treasure?

Stepping Stones

▶ This is a game for 2 or 3 players. You will need coloured counters and six-sided dice. Each player throws the dice to decide where they start the game. If any player throws the same number as another player, keep throwing until you get a different number.

▶ On your turn, throw the dice and multiply by either 2 or 3. If that number is on a nearby stepping stone, you may move your counter there. (You may move horizontally, vertically or diagonally.)

▶ Take it in turns to do this. Two counters may sit on the same square.

▶ The winner is the first person to reach the other side of the river. To extend the game you could try to reach the other side and back again!

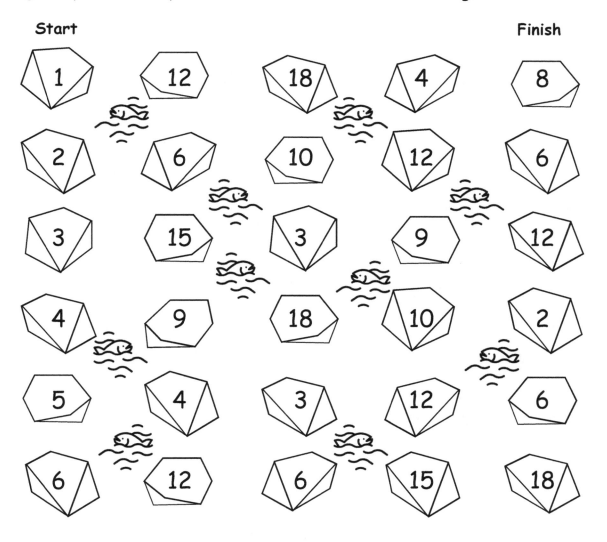

Tables Shading

Shade the numbers in the grid according to the following rules:

Numbers in the 3 times table shade red

Numbers in the 4 times table shade blue

Numbers in the 5 times table shade yellow

9	21	2	29	34	1	37	16	28
11	33	22	7	35	46	14	19	4
3	27	23	25	5	50	13	8	44
18	41	31	17	10	22	7	38	32
33	6	19	14	26	11	23	28	16

What is the answer?

Challenge!

In the following questions assume that each times table goes up to 12×

▶ Look at the red numbers. Are there any numbers in the 3 times table which are not on the grid? Why do you think this is?

▶ Which numbers in the 4 times table are not on the grid and why?

▶ Which numbers in the 5 times table are not on the grid and why?

Make a Face!

▶ This is a game for 2 or 3 players. Players need paper and two six-sided dice.

▶ The aim of the game is to be the first to draw a complete face with mouth, nose, two eyes, two ears and hair.

▶ Players each draw a face outline, then take it in turns to throw the dice and make a 2-digit number. For example, if you throw a 2 and a 4, you could make 24 or 42.

▶ You can now choose to draw one bit of your face as follows:

Throw an even number and you can draw one eye.

Throw an odd number and you can draw one ear.

Throw a number in the 3× table and you can draw the nose.

Throw a number in the 4× table and you can draw the mouth.

Throw a number in the 5× table and you can draw the hair.

▶ Each time you have a turn you can only draw one item. So, if you threw a 24 you could choose to draw an eye, a nose or a mouth. If you already have each of those you can't draw anything.

▶ The winner is the first player to have a face with 2 eyes, 2 ears, nose, mouth and hair.

 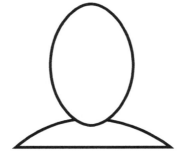 

Aliens

Three aliens are trapped on Earth! Your task is to lead them on a path from Earth though space to find a way out of our galaxy.

Use the following clues to help you:

> **Red Alien must start on 2 and keep adding 2's.**
>
> **Blue Alien must start on 3 and keep adding 3's.**
>
> **Green Alien must start on 5 and keep adding 5's.**

Aliens may travel from square to square horizontally, vertically or diagonally. On the grid, shade a path for each alien in its own colour.

54	25	50	41	3	6	15	38	36	23	64	4	15	2	4
11	34	9	17	37	11	7	25	35	33	30	27	19	13	6
24	70	38	16	18	27	29	13	17	37	41	13	24	7	19
42	22	20	43	15	22	9	15	11	4	19	40	23	21	17
20	23	7	18	21	49	17	112	6	20	34	29	13	18	11
19	11	16	15	13	11	5	3	2	3	6	9	19	15	16
31	14	47	23	7	2				15	80	13	12	11	13
23	12	17	31	4	15				28	44	56	70	19	14
29	41	10	37	6	5				18	19	7	16	3	40
4	7	13	8	11	25	14	4	5	17	40	11	13	29	16
8	49	25	19	30	6	11	10	3	13	27	15	40	49	23
23	47	11	17	50	29	13	23	15	20	25	10	35	45	23
10	8	45	35	13	31	17	11	19	41	37	30	7	50	31
12	6	16	18	19	15	6	18	29	20	15	5	35	55	41
20	4	2	6	7	3	12	9	35	7	29	4	37	13	60

Animal Arithmetic

Each question has an answer which is an animal or insect. First do the calculation, then use the grid below to replace each digit of your answer by a letter.

0	1	2	3	4	5	6	7	8	9
T	C	A	B	E	R	G	D	W	O

1. 3 x 40

answer			
word			

2. 4 x 80

answer			
word			

3. 2 x 260

answer			
word			

4. 99 x 2

answer			
word			

5. 2 x 242

answer			
word			

6. 4 x 86

answer			
word			

7. 4 x 199

answer			
word			

Challenge!

Make up multiplication clues for **goat** and **crow**.

Remainder Shading

Work out the remainders after the following divisions and shade the boxes in according to these rules:

Remainder 1 – red **Remainder 2 – green** **Remainder 3 – blue**

8÷3	9÷7	12÷5	3÷1	8÷4	10÷7	8÷2	11÷7	1÷1	6÷2	13÷9	8÷7	2÷2	5÷2
9÷9	12÷6	14÷4	15÷5	16÷6	18÷9	4÷4	10÷5	6÷6	12÷3	9÷5	3÷2	15÷3	7÷3
14÷3	6÷4	11÷3	9÷1	8÷5	11÷4	7÷4	8÷8	9÷3	7÷6	4÷2	9÷4	5÷1	6÷5
11÷9	4÷1	6÷3	5÷5	12÷8	6÷2	2÷1	14÷7	9÷2	5÷4	4÷3	7÷2	10÷2	10÷3
10÷4	17÷3	7÷5	12÷4	8÷1	13÷5	12÷2	10÷6	6÷1	11÷5	3÷3	15÷5	7÷7	9÷8

What is the remainder?

Hair Share

Miss Summer's class of 24 pupils have brown, black, blonde or red hair as follows:

▶ Half of the class have brown hair

▶ One quarter of the class have blonde hair.

▶ One sixth of the class have red hair.

▶ The rest of the class have black hair.

Colour in the hair of Miss Summer's class:

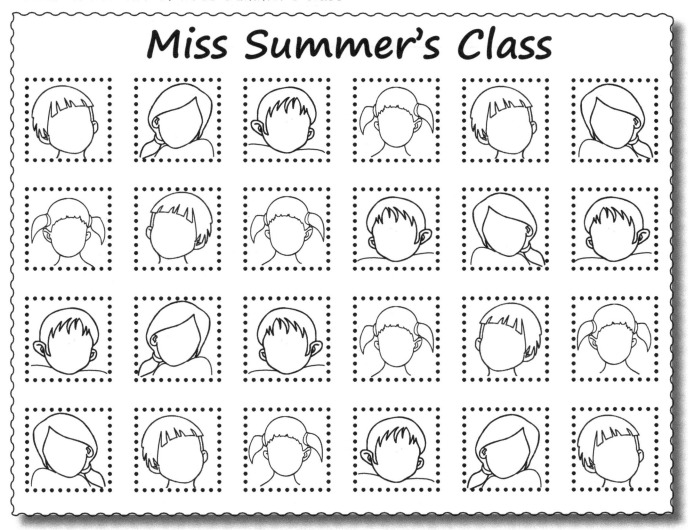

How many pupils have black hair?

What fraction of the class have black hair?

Fractions Shading

Work out the answers in the boxes and shade them in according to the following rules:

- **If the answer is 2, shade the box red**
- **If the answer is 3, shade the box yellow**
- **If the answer is 4, shade the box blue**

$\frac{1}{2}$ of 12	$\frac{1}{2}$ of 6	$\frac{1}{5}$ of 5
$\frac{1}{3}$ of 30	$\frac{1}{5}$ of 15	$\frac{1}{3}$ of 15
$\frac{1}{2}$ of 2	$\frac{1}{3}$ of 9	$\frac{1}{2}$ of 20
$\frac{1}{5}$ of 50	$\frac{1}{10}$ of 30	$\frac{1}{8}$ of 8
$\frac{1}{2}$ of 10	$\frac{1}{4}$ of 12	$\frac{1}{5}$ of 30
$\frac{1}{4}$ of 24	$\frac{1}{6}$ of 6	$\frac{1}{3}$ of 3
$\frac{1}{3}$ of 12	$\frac{1}{2}$ of 8	$\frac{1}{4}$ of 16
$\frac{1}{6}$ of 60	$\frac{1}{4}$ of 20	$\frac{1}{3}$ of 18
$\frac{1}{5}$ of 10	$\frac{1}{3}$ of 6	$\frac{1}{2}$ of 4
$\frac{1}{4}$ of 4	$\frac{1}{5}$ of 25	$\frac{1}{10}$ of 20
$\frac{1}{2}$ of 4	$\frac{1}{4}$ of 8	$\frac{1}{6}$ of 12
$\frac{1}{8}$ of 16	$\frac{1}{10}$ of 10	$\frac{1}{4}$ of 40
$\frac{1}{3}$ of 6	$\frac{1}{5}$ of 10	$\frac{1}{4}$ of 8

What is your answer?

Draw a sketch to represent it.

Party Places

Penny invites 15 friends to her party. They sit around one big table.

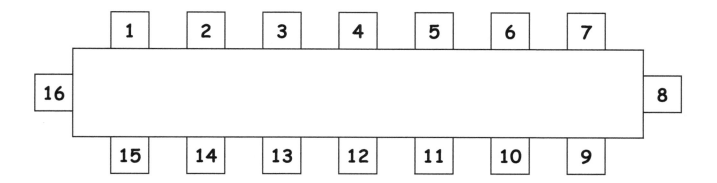

Use these clues to work out where each person is sitting.

▶ Alice is sitting opposite Harry. Alice's number is 3 times Harry's.

▶ Sarah and Kate are sitting next to each other. Their numbers add to 27.

▶ Em's number is half of Sarah's.

▶ Alex is sitting opposite Sasha. Their numbers multiply to give 60. Sasha's number is greater than Alex's.

▶ Megan and Poppy are sitting next to each other. Their numbers multiply to give 6. Poppy's number is odd.

▶ Rob is sitting opposite Mary. Mary's number is half of Rob's.

▶ Will's number is 3 times Mat's.

▶ Joe's number is 8 more than Anna's.

Where does Penny sit?

Make up a clue for Penny.

Threes

◆ This is a game for 2 players

◆ Cut out the number cards and shuffle them.

◆ Shuffle the number cards and deal 12 out face up in front of each player.

◆ Put the remaining number cards in a pile.

◆ Now deal out all of the operations cards.

◆ Player take it in turns to place down number statements on a piece of paper, writing the '=' sign themselves.

For example

If I had the cards 2, 4, 8 and ×, I could place down:

2	×	4	=	8

◆ If a player cannot make a statement they must pick another number card from the pile.

◆ Players continue until one player has played all their cards or there are no more number cards in the pile.

◆ The winner is the first player to have no cards left or the player with the least cards remaining when there are no cards left in the pile.

Number Cards

1	2	3	4	5
1	2	3	4	5
6	6	8	8	9
10	12	12	14	15
16	18	20	20	21
24	24	25	30	40

Operations Cards

+	+	+	+	-
-	-	-	×	×
×	÷	÷	÷	

Wizard Maths

Mervin, the mathematical wizard, makes up some number spells.
Try each spell on 3 different numbers and work out what each spell does.

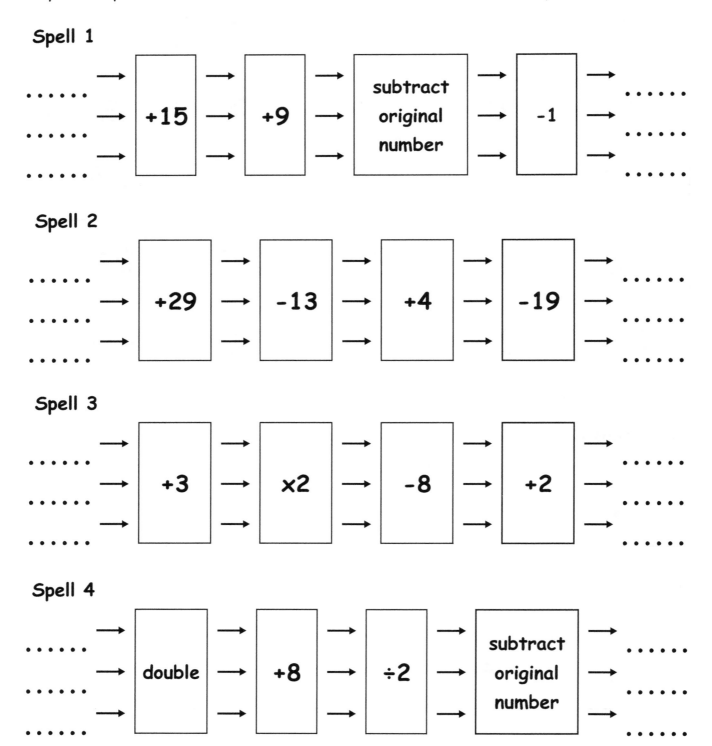

Spell 1

→ | +15 | → | +9 | → | subtract original number | → | -1 | →

Spell 2

→ | +29 | → | -13 | → | +4 | → | -19 | →

Spell 3

→ | +3 | → | x2 | → | -8 | → | +2 | →

Spell 4

→ | double | → | +8 | → | ÷2 | → | subtract original number | →

Four-in-a-line

▶ This is a game for 2 to 3 players.

▶ Throw a 6-sided dice and remember the number

▶ Choose one of the four options above the playing grid to make a new number.

▶ Find your new number on the playing grid and shade it in your colour.

▶ If a player makes a number which has already been shaded, miss a go.

▶ The winner is the first player to shade in a line of 4 (horizontal, vertical or diagonal).

Choose one of these:

Double	Halve	Subtract from 10	Multiply by 3

Playing Grid

1	10	4	3	6
4	18	12	8	10
6	9	7	1	15
2	11	15	5	9
3	8	6	2	12

When you have played the game, try to find the one number in the grid that can never be shaded.

Answers

► Make Ten (p.4)

The lines of 3 numbers adding to 10 make the following picture of a stickman:

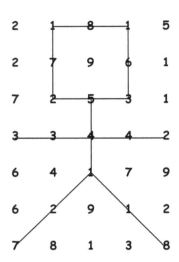

Challenge

The possibilities are: 1,1,8   1,2,7   1,3,6   1,4,5
2,2,6   2,3,5   2,4,4   3,3,4

► Make Twenty (p.5)

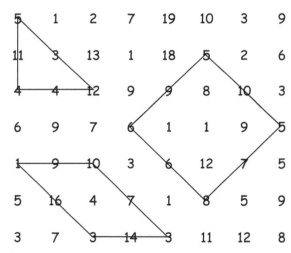

The shapes are right-angled triangle, parallelogram, square.
Challenge There are 33 ways.

► Celebrity Dance! (p.6)

A. The missing numbers for each celebrity are:

1. 21   2. 28   3. 9   4. 6   5. 10

B. The scores for each celebrity are:

1. 8,8,8,8   2. 6,6,6,7   3. 5,7,7,7   4. 1,3,5,7   5. 2,4,6,8

Addition Grids (p.7)

A

+	3	6	5	8
2	5	8	7	10
7	10	13	12	15
9	12	15	14	17
4	7	10	9	12

B

+	9	6	3	8
4	13	10	7	12
5	14	11	8	13
7	16	13	10	15
2	11	8	5	10

C

+	2	6	8	4
9	11	15	17	13
7	9	13	15	11
3	5	9	11	7
5	7	11	13	9

Challenge: All the numbers are odd. This is because the numbers along the left are all odd and the numbers across the top are all even. Therefore, each number inside the grid is the sum of an odd number and an even number. An odd number and an even number always add to make an odd number.

▶ Colour the Number (p.8)

Challenge:

1. 3,9   4,8   5,7

2. No she can't, because it is impossible to throw the number 1 with two dice.

3. It is best to colour the '9'. There are less opportunities to colour big numbers as you have to throw larger numbers on the dice. Smaller numbers can be used in lots of different combinations and so have greater flexibility.

▶ Sum Arrows (p.9)

A.

46	→	66	→	86	→	106	→	126		→ +20
42	→	62	→	82	→	102	→	122		↑ +4
38	→	58	→	78	→	98	→	118		
34	→	54	→	74	→	94	→	114		
30	→	50	→	70	→	90	→	110		

(↑ arrows connect each row upward)

B.

35	→	65	→	95	→	125	→	155		→ +30
28	→	58	→	88	→	118	→	148		↑ +7
21	→	51	→	81	→	111	→	141		
14	→	44	→	74	→	104	→	134		
7	→	37	→	67	→	97	→	127		

▶ Wizard Maze (p.10)

The answers to each question are shown below. The way out is at number 37.

3→22 → 50→ 13→ 61→ 39→57→ 41→ 60→ 43→ 72→ 57→ 43→ 87→

69 → 31→ 70→ 46→54→ 36→ 14→ 51→24→ 76→ 37

▶ Sums and Differences (p.11)

Answers are shaded. In questions 6, 7, 8, 9 answers may be either way round.

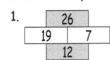
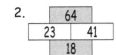

1. | 26 |
   | 19 | 7 |
   | 12 |

2. | 64 |
   | 23 | 41 |
   | 18 |

3. | 85 |
   | 49 | 36 |
   | 13 |

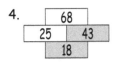

4. | 68 |
   | 25 | 43 |
   | 18 |

5. | 77 |
   | 59 | 18 |
   | 41 |

6. | 10 |
   | 7 | 3 |
   | 4 |

7. | 15 |
   | 8 | 7 |
   | 1 |

8. | 30 |
   | 18 | 12 |
   | 6 |

9. | 100 |
   | 75 | 25 |
   | 50 |

▶ Find a Fiver (p.12)

The correct arrangement is: F E B

C G A

D I H

▶ Sequences (p.13)

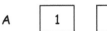   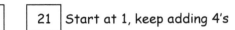

A | 1 | 5 | 9 | **13** | 17 | 21 | Start at 1, keep adding 4's

B | 5 | **7** | 9 | 11 | 13 | 15 | Start at 5, keep adding 2's

C | 3 | 11 | **19** | 27 | 35 | 43 | Start at 3, keep adding 8's

D | 6 | **10** | 14 | 18 | 22 | 26 | Start at 6, keep adding 4's

E | 8 | 10 | 12 | 14 | **16** | 18 | Start at 8, keep adding 2's

F | **4** | 9 | 14 | 19 | 24 | 29 | Start at 4, keep adding 5's

The shaded numbers make the sequence: 4, 7, 10, 13, 16, 19 so next 3 terms are 22, 25, 28.

▶ Treasure Hunt (p.14)

One-eye Guy: 3, 8, 13, 18, 23, 28, 33
Captain Cath: 0, 7, 14, 21, 28, 35, 42
Blonde Beard: 6, 8, 10, 12, 14, 16, 18, 20, 22, 24
Toothless Tina: 24, 20, 16, 12, 8, 4, 0
Cut-throat Ken: 9, 12, 15, 18, 21, 24, 27

Challenge: The pirate will never reach the treasure!
The sequence is 5, 7, 9, 11, 13,
... so only ever goes through odd numbers. Therefore, 18 can never be reached.

Answers (cont.)

▶ Tables Shading (p.16)

9	21	2	29	34	1	37	16	28
11	33	22	7	35	46	14	19	4
3	27	23	25	5	50	13	8	44
18	41	31	17	10	22	7	38	32
33	6	19	14	26	11	23	28	16

↑ red   ↑ yellow   ↑ blue

Challenge:

The numbers in the 3× table not on the grid are 12, 15, 24, 30, 36. This is because they are also in either the 4 or 5× table, so pupils would not know which colour to make them.

Numbers in 4× table not there are 12, 20, 24, 36, 40, 48 as they are also in the 3 or 5× tables.

Numbers in 5× table not there are 15, 20, 30, 40, 45, 60 as they are also in the 3 or 4× tables.

▶ Aliens (p.18)

54	25	50	41	3	6	15	38	36	23	64	4	15	2	4
11	34	9	17	37	11	7	25	35	33	30	27	19	13	6
24	70	38	16	18	27	29	13	17	37	41	13	24	7	19
42	22	20	43	15	22	9	15	11	4	19	40	23	21	17
20	23	7	18	21	49	17	112	6	20	34	29	13	18	11
19	11	16	15	13	11	5	3	2	3	6	9	19	15	16
31	14	47	23	7	2				15	80	13	12	11	13
23	12	17	31	4	15				28	44	56	70	19	14
29	41	10	37	6	5				18	19	7	16	3	40
4	7	13	8	11	25	14	4	5	17	40	11	13	29	16
8	49	25	19	30	6	11	10	3	13	27	15	40	49	23
23	47	11	17	50	29	13	23	15	20	25	10	35	45	23
10	8	45	35	13	31	17	11	19	41	37	30	7	50	31
12	6	16	18	19	15	6	18	29	20	15	5	35	55	41
20	4	2	6	7	3	12	9	35	7	29	4	37	13	60

Red Alien: 2, 4, 6, 8, 10, 12, 14, 16, 18, 20, 22, 24

Blue Alien: 3, 6, 9, 12, 15, 18, 21, 24, 27, 30, 33, 36

Green Alien: 5, 10, 15, 20, 25, 30, 35, 40, 45, 50, 55, 60

▶ Animal Arithmetic (p.19)

	Answer	Word
1.	120	CAT
2.	320	BAT
3.	520	RAT
4.	198	COW
5.	484	EWE
6.	344	BEE
7.	796	DOG

Answers (cont.)

▶ **Remainder Shading** (p.20)

5÷2	2÷2	8÷7	13÷9	6÷2	1÷1	11÷7	8÷2	10÷7	8÷4	3÷1	12÷5	9÷7	8÷3
7÷3	15÷3	3÷2	9÷5	12÷3	6÷6	10÷5	4÷4	18÷9	16÷6	15÷5	14÷4	12÷6	9÷9
6÷5	5÷1	9÷4	4÷2	7÷6	9÷3	8÷8	7÷4	11÷4	8÷5	9÷1	11÷3	6÷4	14÷3
10÷3	10÷2	7÷2	4÷3	5÷4	9÷2	14÷7	2÷1	6÷2	12÷8	5÷5	6÷3	4÷1	11÷9
9÷8	7÷7	13÷5	3÷3	11÷5	6÷1	10÷6	12÷2	13÷5	8÷1	12÷4	7÷5	17÷3	10÷4

↑ red   ↑ red   ↑ blue   ↑ green

14 ÷ 5 leaves a remainder of 4

▶ **Hair Share** (p.21)

12 with brown hair, 6 with blonde hair, 4 with red hair, so 2 have black hair ($\frac{1}{12}$).

▶ **Fractions Shading** (p.22)

The answer is $\frac{1}{2}$

$\frac{1}{2}$ of 12	$\frac{1}{2}$ of 6	$\frac{1}{5}$ of 5	
$\frac{1}{3}$ of 30	$\frac{1}{5}$ of 15	$\frac{1}{3}$ of 15	→ yellow
$\frac{1}{2}$ of 2	$\frac{1}{3}$ of 9	$\frac{1}{2}$ of 20	
$\frac{1}{5}$ of 50	$\frac{1}{10}$ of 30	$\frac{1}{8}$ of 8	
$\frac{1}{2}$ of 10	$\frac{1}{4}$ of 12	$\frac{1}{5}$ of 30	
$\frac{1}{4}$ of 24	$\frac{1}{6}$ of 6	$\frac{1}{3}$ of 3	
$\frac{1}{3}$ of 12	$\frac{1}{2}$ of 8	$\frac{1}{4}$ of 16	→ blue
$\frac{1}{6}$ of 60	$\frac{1}{4}$ of 20	$\frac{1}{3}$ of 18	
$\frac{1}{5}$ of 10	$\frac{1}{3}$ of 6	$\frac{1}{2}$ of 4	
$\frac{1}{4}$ of 4	$\frac{1}{5}$ of 25	$\frac{1}{10}$ of 20	
$\frac{1}{2}$ of 4	$\frac{1}{4}$ of 8	$\frac{1}{6}$ of 12	→ red
$\frac{1}{8}$ of 16	$\frac{1}{10}$ of 10	$\frac{1}{4}$ of 40	
$\frac{1}{3}$ of 6	$\frac{1}{5}$ of 10	$\frac{1}{4}$ of 8	

▶ **Party Places** (p.23)

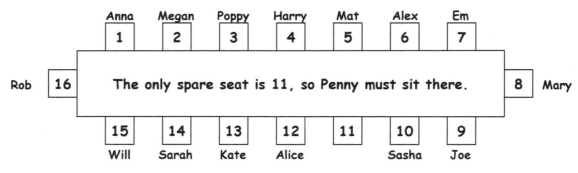

The only spare seat is 11, so Penny must sit there.

Anna	Megan	Poppy	Harry	Mat	Alex	Em
1	2	3	4	5	6	7

Rob 16   8 Mary

15	14	13	12	11	10	9
Will	Sarah	Kate	Alice		Sasha	Joe

▶ **Wizard Maths** (p.26)

Spell 1: always gives answer 23.   **Spell 2:** adds 1 to the original number.
Spell 3: doubles the original number. **Spell 4:** always gives answer 4.

▶ **Four-in-a-line** (p.27): Number 11 can never be shaded.

Answers (cont.)

Lightning Source UK Ltd.
Milton Keynes UK
UKHW05f1831300818
328061UK00003B/11/P